PENNY TOOGOOD

Hope Full

GW00471174

Contents

1

A blank sheet of paper

'Do not remember the former things, Nor consider the things of old. Behold, I will do a new thing, Now it shall spring forth; Shall you not know it? I will even make a road in the wilderness. And rivers in the desert'.

Isaiah 43:18-21

Every birthday and Christmas one of the things at the top of my girls list of presents is a new notebook. Despite the fact that they have a ton of notebooks in their bedrooms there appears to be nothing more satisfying than opening up a new page and starting with a clean sheet of paper on which they love to put all their new ideas, pictures and stories. The first page always has the neatest handwriting, it's like a fresh start. Many of you probably understand that feeling, we even have phrases *'like turning over a new leaf'*, or *'starting with a blank sheet of paper'*. We all love the opportunity to start afresh. This is not a bad thing. In fact it is what the Lord actually encourages us to do. In today's verse we see the Lord calling his people to lift up their eyes, to see into the future and to begin to believe for a new thing that he is going to do among them.

The Lord does not want us to be stuck in failure, sin or discouragement from the past. That is why he tells us *"Do not remember the former things, Nor consider the things of old."* He understands that if we dwell on these we will stay defeated and we will never be able to move forward into the new things that he has for us. When we read Isaiah 43 we learn that it is not that the Lord wants us to ignore the past and act like it never happened. In fact in verses 16-17 he tells Israel to look to the past and remember the great things God did for them at the Red Sea. You see, our view of the past needs to be through the lens of God's love and faithfulness towards us. The Lord wants us to remember the incredible works He has done for us. He wants us to be mindful of His goodness and recognise His hand of deliverance and provision. However he doesn't want us to pay attention to our shortcomings and where we mess up because this will hold us back from believing that there is hope for tomorrow.

Biblical hope is not like hope that the world talks about. Worldly hope is based on our ability to perform but biblical hope is a confident expectation of good based not on our efforts but on the faithfulness of the Lord. In these verses Isaiah was prophesying of a time when the Israelites would be released from exile. He was talking to God's people who were being held in captivity in Babylon. The Lord promises that *"I will even make a road in the wilderness."* For God's people at that time they were separated from their homeland by literally hundreds of miles of desert and yet the Lord was telling them that although all they could see was the impossibility of the situation He would provide a way through. He wanted them to see with eyes of faith into the future that He had prepared for them.

Today we might be struggling to lay hold of promises in our lives because we are overwhelmed by the obstacles that we can see ahead of us. We are forgetting that the Lord has made us *"more than conquerors"* (Romans

8:37). The Lord wants us to step back and recognise that He is going before us and making a way. He is working behind the scenes of our lives and He is making plans that we know nothing about.

Today our responsibility is to let go of our burdens and to leave our problems in His capable hands.

2

Be Prepared!

'Thus King Rehoboam strengthened himself in Jerusalem and reigned. Now Rehoboam was forty-one years old when he became king; and he reigned seventeen years in Jerusalem, ... And he did evil, because he did not prepare his heart to seek the LORD'.

2 Chronicles 12:13-14

"Be prepared" was the motto of the scouting movement and it is a phrase that has served many people well over the years as they have learnt the value of thinking ahead and planning for the unexpected. When we think of preparing ourselves we are often concerned with the practical issues of life. The physical things that we will need before we go on a trip away. The arrangements and logistics that are required to ensure that everything will run smoothly. One of things that we sometimes neglect is the inner work. How prepared are we for the challenges of life? How much time have we taken to equip ourselves to face down trials and come out fitter and stronger on the other side?

King Rehoboam was King Solomon's son. He inherited incredible wealth and yet we find that within 5 years of his rule he is attacked by Egypt and he ends up losing most of his financial resources. *'When Shishak, king of Egypt attacked Jerusalem, he carried off the treasures of the temple of the Lord and the treasures of the royal palace. He took everything, including the gold shields Solomon had made'* (2 Chronicles 12:9).

Now according to experts the shields alone are estimated to have a worth today of around 50 million pounds! So why is it that things went so badly for Rehoboam? What lessons can we learn from his life? What mistakes did he make that we can avoid today?

It tells us at the start of the chapter that *"After Rehoboam's position as king was established and he had become strong, he and all Israel with him abandoned the law of the Lord."* (2 Chronicles 12:1).

Rehoboam failed to see that the position he had inherited was not as a result of his strength or ability but it was given to him by the Lord. When Rehoboam trusted in his own efforts he became proud and he then suffered the effects of turning away from God. It's easy for us to look with hindsight and think how foolish he was to make such a choice. But I believe there are times when we can all trust in our strength and attribute our success to our efforts and hard work.

I believe the key to all of this is found in verse 14, *'And he did evil, because he did not prepare his heart to seek the LORD'.* Rehoboam had not decided early on in his life who he would turn to for wisdom, strength, direction and fulfilment. He allowed his heart to be easily swayed by outward circumstances. When he became strong and secure in his reign as King he forsook the ways of the Lord.

Although he did realise the error of his ways and repent, his life followed a very turbulent path and he only turned to the Lord when life was not going well. There was no dependence and connection with God, it was rather a cry for help when he was in a tight spot. Unlike his grandfather David, he did not have a relationship with the Lord where his heart was surrendered to following God's will. He did not prepare himself by taking time to seek the Lord and allow the Lord to shape his heart and do a deep work within him. Therefore when pressure came he could not stand strong and he made poor decisions.

The Lord wants us to learn today to prepare ourselves and set our minds on His ways. To be steadfast about where we will place our trust. Do not look at your success and become less dependent on the Lord but rather look at your success and thank the Him for his incredible blessings and favour in your life. When you do this you can have confidence and hope for your future!

3

The Lord longs to lead us

"My heart is fixed, O God, my heart is fixed: I will sing and give praise. Awake up, my glory; awake, psaltery and harp: I myself will awake early. I will praise thee, O Lord, among the people: I will sing unto thee among the nations. For thy mercy is great unto the heavens, and thy truth unto the clouds. Be thou exalted, O God, above the heavens: let thy glory be above all the earth".

Psalm 57:7-11

Do you find there are times in life when you feel that you are crippled with indecision? You know that you need to make a choice but out of fear or confusion you just can't seem to have the courage to call it either one way or the other. This feeling of being in limbo can be very unsettling and it is not actually what the Lord desires for us. The Lord is our shepherd and as such He is our guide. He wants us to trust him and to be led by him, even when we don't understand exactly how it is all going to work out or precisely where we are heading.

Look at David's life. He had an incredible promise from the Lord that he would be King. He had been anointed by Samuel the prophet and then everything in his life appears to go in the opposite direction. Yet David managed to put his faith and trust in the Lord despite what he was experiencing. *"My heart is fixed, O God, my heart is fixed: I will sing and give praise."* David spoke these words during the time that Saul was trying to hunt him down and kill him. It's often easy to say we love the Lord and we will follow him all our days when things are going well. It's another thing to be praising God when you are running for your life. But this was the key to David's success. This was why the Lord was able to promote him and trust him to lead the nation and become King. David was not swayed by his circumstances. He had decided in his heart whom he would serve and he remained faithful.

If we examine the word "fixed" we find that the original word is *Kuwn* which means "prepared, fixed, firmly in position, not subject to change or variation." The point of something that is fixed is that it is set in place before it is needed. Think of abseilers coming down a mountain. They fix a knot in a rope before they put any weight on the cord. They wouldn't think of trying to tie a knot as they are careering off the edge of the slope. They ensure everything is firmly fastened then they can have confidence that as pressure is applied the cord will hold because the knot is securely in place.

This is true of us as we journey through life and navigate our way over obstacles and hurdles that stand in our path. We need to set our hearts on a course of action before something happens – then we will not fall away. We are often really good at reactionary prayer but the Lord wants to encourage us to have our hearts set on Him at all times so that we are prepared for any and every situation. Unless you set your heart on a course of action you will drift.

Today make sure that your eyes are firmly fixed on the Lord. Let your heart be filled with His word. Build your foundations in his love and goodness towards you. When you do, you will be ready to, *"walk through the valley of baca (weeping) and it will become a place of refreshing springs. The autumn rains will clothe it with blessings."* (Psalm 84:6).

4

Just let go!

'Stand fast therefore in the liberty by which Christ has made us free, and do not be entangled again with a yoke of bondage'.

Galations 5:1

I remember as a child going on a family day out with my grandparents. There was great excitement as my grandfather had made a kite and we were going out to fly it. My older brother was allowed to go first and we all watched in amazement as the kite soared into the air. After much persuasion the grown ups finally gave in and let me have a turn. I was given an endless list of instructions and told repeatedly "whatever you do, just hold on tight, even if it pulls a little, don't let go." You probably already know the end to the story! There was a big gush of wind, the kite rose high into the air, the strings tightened and I thought I was going to be transported halfway across the world so I panicked and let go of the kite. It shot off into the sky and disappeared into the a nearby forest, never to be seen again!

What I learnt that day was that holding on is not easy. Even standing still can be difficult. Just watch any toddler in a queue. It's practically impossible. So if standing still in the natural is so hard for us, how can we be expected to stand fast when it comes to spiritual issues? Surely we are just setting ourselves up to fail? Are we not going to end up being pulled in all directions unable to hold on?

The answer is, of course, that the Lord is not expecting us to have it all together. He knows how easily we can fall and how our best efforts often fail. So what exactly is he asking us to do when he exhorts us to *stand fast.* The original word here for stand is *"steko,"* which means to be stationary, or to be still. This stillness is echoed for us in Psalm 46 where we read *"be still and know that I am God."* The Hebrew word for *"still"* here is *"harpu,"* meaning to let go, to surrender or to relax. It comes from the root word *"rafa"* which means to rest. As we pull all this together can we get a clearer picture of what the Lord is saying to us when he calls us to stand fast.

Rather than our self -effort and our determination to hold our ground, the Lord is showing us a much simpler way that does not depend on our performance but relies solely on his grace. He does not want us to "grit our teeth" and "hold on come what may," instead He wants us to let go and surrender, to relax and sink into his arms. He wants us to know that He is holding us as we settle ourselves, as we remain stationary and still we can have confidence that we are sinking into his grace.

As Galatians 5:1 tells us - **'Christ delivered us into freedom'.** We no longer have to carry the weight and burden in life. He has taken all the responsibility on his shoulders and we can enjoy a life knowing that we no longer need to be in control. We can rely instead on the fact that the Lord is taking care of us. All our failures from the past are covered by his grace through the blood of Jesus. All our tomorrows are secure because He is going before us, and preparing good days for us to enjoy. So right in this moment we can be still, we can be stationary, trusting and believing that as we let go and surrender He is giving us the grace and strength that we need for our hearts to be at peace and rest.

5

No More Fear!

'The Lord is my light and my salvation; Whom shall I fear? The Lord is the strength of my life, Of whom shall I be afraid'?

Psalm 27:1,2

S tudies have shown that one of the biggest issues in the health profession today is not poor nutrition or lack of exercise - it is actually worry. We all understand the effects of a bad diet and a poor exercise routine but many of us don't take the time to really consider the implications of a negative thought life. Why is worrying such a problem and how do we tackle it?

Worry is rooted in fear. The reason that it has such a damaging effect on us is due to the fact that we were not built for fear, we were built for love. Toxic thinking damages our minds and puts a stress on our bodies that we were not designed to cope with. We were created to depend on the Lord and to expect him to take care of all of our needs. When we operate independently of him we take on pressures and burdens that we were never intended to carry and we find ourselves overwhelmed.

Love is the currency of God's kingdom. He is love itself. He only operates in love and as we are made in his image we are made to operate in love not fear. So why is it that so many of us believers are trapped in the same debilitating thought patterns like people in the world when we are called to a life of freedom? The word tells us that " *perfect love casts out fear.*" Now we know that the only one who can love perfectly is Jesus so when we know Jesus and his perfect love for us we will find that fear is driven out of our hearts.

In today's verse we see how King David although writing this psalm before Jesus walked the earth had a relationship with his heavenly Father in which he experienced this depth of love. Because of this he was able to walk with assurance and peace and not allow circumstances to overwhelm his heart with fear and worry. We know from David's life that he was a man who was familiar with danger. He spent many years in hiding, having to flee for his life from King Saul. He had many obstacles and challenges and at times wrestled with negative emotions, but David prevailed because he knew the Lord as his *"light and salvation."* When David was confused he cried out to the Lord for answers and the Lord illuminated his mind and showed him a way out. When David was surrounded the Lord delivered him and when David was faced with a giant (literally) the Lord gave him strength.

You see even though David was a skilled and experienced warrior who would have had considerable physical strength his trust was not in his own ability but in the Lord's. He looked to the Lord to supply his needs. He relied on the Lord to deliver him and he called on the Lord for help. He repeatedly saw the Lord's faithfulness and because of this he had confidence that there was no need to fear or be afraid. The Lord was the strength of his life.

Today our hope is in the Lord and him alone. Too often we put our trust in our wisdom, our experience, our friends, and our resources. As we read about David's life and how he trusted in the Lord we can have confidence about our tomorrows. The word tells us that "God is no respecter of persons." If he delivered David from Goliath and Saul and kept his promise to make him king and establish his kingdom, then the Lord will be faithful to the promises he has spoken over your life. Choose to trust in his word and know that you can rely on his light to lead you, his hand to deliver you and his strength to make you more than a conqueror in every situation you face.

As David says : *'In this I shall be confident!" V3.* So go forward today and *"Be strong in the Lord and in the power of his might!"* (Ephesians 6:10).

6

Walking in Peace, Joy and Hope

'I would have lost heart, unless I had believed that I would see the goodness of the Lord in the land of the living'.

Psalm 27:13

Have you ever had moments when you have felt like giving up? Have there been times when you have wondered what's the point of it all? Why try because it never changes? When we begin to struggle with these thoughts we need to ask ourselves where they are coming from or perhaps more accurately who they are coming from. They could be coming from our own hurt and disappointment or it could be the enemy bringing discouragement. One thing we can be certain of is that they are not from the Lord.

The bible clearly tells us that hope is from God. In fact in Romans Paul says; *"May the God of hope fill you with all joy and peace in faith so that you overflow with hope by the power of the Holy Spirit."* (Romans 15:13). This is the Lord's will and desire for us. That hope would bubble up within us to the point that we can't contain it and it actually becomes contagious and affects the people around us. So how can we walk in this joy, peace and hope? This verse explains to us that filling us with hope is the Lord's work. It is not something that we can do by our own efforts. It's not about trying to be hopeful. It's recognising that hope comes from the Lord and that when we commune with him a by product will be that we will be filled with hope, peace and joy.

Being filled with hope is the work of the Holy Spirit in your life. As you take time and meditate on the word *"the Helper, the Holy Spirit, whom the Father will send in my name, he will teach you all things and bring to your remembrance all that I have said to you"* (John 14:26). He will remind you of all the good things the Lord has done. He will show you the Lord's faithfulness, the Lord's goodness, the Lord's salvation and the Lord's strength. He will point to times in your own life where the Lord has come through for you and He will fill your mind with the miraculous acts throughout scripture where his people were delivered, set free and given a second chance. Paul goes on to tell us in (Romans 15:4) that *"whatever things were written before were written for our learning, that we through the patience and comfort of the Scriptures might have hope."* The word is full of hope and promises for the future. It is impossible to read it and dwell on it and to remain the same.

David in Psalm 27 found that as he waited on the Lord he found courage and strength. For him waiting was not a passive action; it was rather a time of aligning his heart back with the truth of who God was and what he had called him for. Many times circumstances can feel like they are going to overwhelm us but the reality is we have allowed them to appear bigger than God. Today we need to remind ourselves of who we belong to. We are sons and daughters of the King of all kings (John 1:12), we are in this world but not of this world (John 17:16). We have an enemy who has been defeated (Col 2:15) and we have been called to reign in life

(Romans 5:17). What is more *"we can come with confidence (and) draw near to the throne of grace, that we may receive mercy and find grace to help in time of need"* (Hebrew 4:16).

As we set our minds on things above and fill them with the reality of heaven we will find that hope rises in our hearts and the negative thoughts no longer have a hold on us. So take time out today, feed on God's word, commune with the Holy Spirit and let the light of Jesus illuminate the scriptures in a fresh way. I guarantee that as we fix our eyes on Jesus we will find that as David showed us " *He shall strengthen your heart.*" (Psalm 27:14).

7

Step out and Believe!

'God also bound himself with an oath, so that those who received the promise could be perfectly sure that he would never change his mind. So God has given both his promise and his oath. These two things are unchangeable because it is impossible for God to lie. Therefore, we who have fled to him for refuge can have great confidence as we hold to the hope that lies before us. This hope is a strong and trustworthy anchor for our souls'.

Hebrews 6:16-19

How confident are you feeling about your life today? How confident are you about your future? Growing in confidence is something that I spend a lot of my time encouraging people around. What I have discovered is we will only become more confident in a particular area of skill when we step out and try it. Confidence is not something that comes outside of experience. Let me explain.

I have coached a lot of people in the last number of years and the one thing they all have in common is this, the more they practice a skill, go for it and give it a try, the more they grow in confidence. Thinking or talking about it doesn't make a big difference. They have to step out and experience it and when they do they realise that it was not as daunting as they thought. The fear lessens, the thoughts of failure wain away and an optimism is born. Suddenly they can see past the impossible and can imagine themselves becoming competent in this new area of life.

I love to see this journey in people! I love to see them develop and realise their potential. To let go of their limited thinking and to believe for more. As I was pondering this I recognised how our confidence in what the Lord says to us grows as we step out and believe his promises and experience his goodness in our lives. Take giving for example. We can hear it preached that the Lord will provide for us, we can read about how the Lord will prosper us, we can meditate on verses about how the Lord will bless his people. But if we fail to step out and follow his principles in the area of generosity we will only have a head knowledge of this. We will never actually experience the fullness of what the Lord has for us because we haven't allowed our confidence to grow in this area. We haven't done something new and seen the results. Therefore we are always left thinking, does this really apply to me? How can I be sure?

The Lord wants us to trust him. He wants us to take him at his word. This verse tells us that it is impossible for God to lie, so what does that mean for us today? He wants us to take hold of his promises over our lives and to anchor our decisions, choices and actions around them. He wants us to step out in faith and go after new opportunities that will stretch us outside of our comfort zones. He wants us to dream big and believe in the incredible potential that He has placed on the inside of each one of us. He wants us to see beyond our resources and to look to our heavenly supply believing for increase in our finances, our influence, our connections and our impact.

We are blessed to be a blessing. We have been built to reveal the glory of the Father in our lives and to point people to the life giving hope that is found in a relationship with Jesus. Are you confident of your calling today? Are you stepping into everything that the Lord has planned for you? Be confident of this. The Lord has set his hope in you. Hebrews 10:23 tells us " Let's hold on to the confession of our hope without wavering, because the one who made the promises is reliable."

There are many voices in our lives today, many people who promise many things, but there is one who is steadfast, assured and whose word lasts forever. His name is Jesus, He is the "trustworthy anchor for our souls." Fix your hope on Him today!

8

A Certain Hope

"The assurance of things hoped for, the conviction of things not seen"

Hebrews 11:1

What are you hoping for today? What are you picturing for your future? You see we probably use the word hope many times everyday. You might say "I hope this deal goes through" or "I hope I pass my exams" or "I hope my kids are going to be safe." When we use the word "hope" in ordinary English vocabulary, it is generally distinguished from certainty. We would say, "I don't know what's going to happen, but I hope it happens." Hope is the desire for something good in the future.

When we look to the scriptures however we find that there is a distinct biblical meaning of hope. The most important feature of biblical hope is not present in any of these ordinary uses of the word hope. In fact, the distinctive meaning of hope in Scripture is almost the opposite of our ordinary usage. It's not that in Scripture hope is a desire for something bad (instead of something good), or that hope is rejection of good (instead of desire for it). It is not the opposite in those senses.

It is the opposite in this sense: ordinarily, when we use the word hope, we express uncertainty rather than certainty. My kids often say "I hope daddy gets home early," this means, "I don't have any certainty that daddy will get home on time, I only desire that he does." "A good tailwind is our only hope of arriving on time," means, "A good tailwind would bring us to our desired destination, but we can't be sure we will get one." Normally, when we express hope, we are expressing uncertainty. Whereas biblical hope is not just a desire for something good in the future, but rather a confident expectation for something good in the future.

Biblical hope not only desires something good for the future but it expects it to happen. And it not only expects it to happen, it is confident that it will happen. There is a certainty that the good we expect, and desire will be done. Biblical hope has confidence, expectation and certainty in it. When the word says, "Hope in God!" it does not mean, "Cross your fingers." It means, to use the words of William Carey, "Expect great things from God."

We see this in the scriptures the whole way through. Let's look at the words that are used in the bible for hope. "*O Israel HOPE in the Lord for with the Lord there is mercy*". Psalm 130:7. Here the word hope is *Yachal* –it means trust and confidence. "*And now Lord, what do I wait for*"? "*My hope is in you.*" Psalm 39:7. Here the word for hope is *towcheleth* it means expectation.

When it comes to the New Testament we see the word used for hope is *Elpis, it means* "to expect, to anticipate with pleasure, to have a strong confident expectation!!" Are you starting to get the picture? It is important that we have a true biblical understanding of what this word means. When we do the scriptures come alive and we begin to experience the heart of the Lord towards us!!

The Lord doesn't want us to be in any doubt of his intentions towards us. He is good and His plans for us are to give us hope. Not a hope that is uncertain in which we are wavering as to whether we can truly depend on it. But the hope that the Lord gives us is steadfast and sure. It is unchanging. It is not swayed by circumstances. It is founded in his character and we know that he is faithful so we can trust his word and believe. Allow this confident expectation of good to fill your heart and step out and believe the promises He has spoken over your life!

9

See your reality as it really is

"Now faith brings our hopes into reality and becomes the foundation needed to acquire the things we long for. It is all the evidence required to prove what is still unseen".

Hebrews 11:1

Many of us have experienced moments or even seasons of hopelessness in our lives. There are times when life overwhelms us and we have the desolating sense that some things can never be fixed. Such times of trial can turn our declaration from the triumphant, "nothing is impossible with God", into a weary "nothing is ever going to change." You might not voice it out loud, but many have come to expect that God will not answer certain prayers, never mind, Isaiah 64:1, *"rend the heavens and come down"*.

It might be sickness, death and loss, a broken marriage, or a broken ministry, where no matter what you do nothing seems to work. Or perhaps just a broken soul, where darkness has driven the light out from you. In the wreckage of that kind of brokenness, we feel justified in adopting a hopeless view of our life. We might even call our hopelessness realism.

The Bible has lots of those "realists" or more accurately - cynical characters. Cynicism is a killer of hope. The Bible has its Sarah's who laugh at God's promise, its Elijah's who have eyes to see only God's enemies and its Thomas' who resign themselves to death. But we are called for more than that. As the people of God, you and I, are a people of hope. We are the kind who lock eyes with our world's fundamental brokenness, size it up from head to toe, and still step into the ring.

Abraham looks at his barren wife and, "*in hope he believed against hope, that he should become the father of many nations*" (Romans 4:18). Ruth turns her eyes from a dead husband to a new country, and tells Naomi, "*Where you go I will go, and where you lodge I will lodge*", (Ruth 1:16). Habakkuk sees the Babylonian hordes coming to destroy his people, and still he sings, "*I will rejoice in the Lord; I will take joy in the God of my salvation*", (Habakkuk 3:18). Micah collapses under the weight of his own sin, and yet he boasts, "*When I fall, I shall rise; when I sit in darkness, the Lord will be a light to me*" (Micah 7:8).

Each one of these people knew what it was to stand neck-deep in brokenness. They felt the tension between God's promises and their seemingly hopeless circumstances. And yet they still chose to hope that God could give "*life to the dead and [call] into existence the things that do not exist*" (Romans 4:17). By faith, they banished despair as they grasped onto "*the assurance of things hoped for, the conviction of things not seen*" (Hebrews 11:1).

In other words, they were people who saw reality as it really is.

Today the Lord says set your hope FULLY on my grace for you. No half measures or holding back. The greatest risk for you and I today is not to trust and believe God for enough! Do you want to reduce the God of the Universe, the all powerful, all mighty, eternal God to the level of our human understanding and personal experience?

We want to walk in hope today. So how do we do this? Hope is a portion or part of faith. Faith and hope are overlapping realities: hope is faith in the future tense. So most of faith is hope. The Bible says *"Faith comes by hearing and hearing by the word of God"* (Romans 10:17). This implies that hope, like faith, is also strengthened by the word of grace. Hope comes from reading his precious and very great promises and looking to Jesus who has made a way for us to walk in them!

10

We are a people of hope

Set your hope fully on the grace that will be brought to you at the revelation of Jesus Christ"

1 Peter 1:13

A re there times you find it difficult to stay in hope? Do you struggle on occasions to believe that God's word applies to your situation? Hope is something that is based on a future event coming to pass and the only assurance that we have that it will indeed happen is a promise. This is where it becomes tricky for us, can we truly believe that it is possible to keep a promise?

Many of us have experienced disappointment from broken promises made by others and we know the frustration we feel towards ourselves when we fail to keep our word or our commitments. With this as our backdrop we can tend to approach the bible and God's words to us with the same caution.

What we need to remember is that when we read the word "hope" in the Bible it is not wishful thinking. It's not "I don't know if it's going to happen, but I hope it happens." Our hope is a confidence that something will come to pass because God has promised it. The reason we can trust is because it's based on Jesus and His grace. Our hope is not in our ability but in His unearned, undeserved and unmerited favour in our lives.

For many believers this is a difficult message to grasp. It's like we want to believe it but we dare not get our "hopes up." There are times that we might think it is better to lower our expectations than to deal with our disappointment if what we are believing for does not come to pass. We do this as a way of protecting ourselves but we actually forfeit the opportunity to enter into the fulness of life that God has planned for us.

Think for a moment about all the amazing stories of faith in the Bible that we read for inspiration. Now take anyone of them - David facing Goliath, Joshua at Jericho, Moses crossing the red sea. How would these stories have read if we placed into them a "don't get your hopes' up" mentality? The Lord commands Joshua to "Be strong and courageous." We have to step out with boldness and put our trust in God's word. The enemy will tell you the lie that you can believe to a level but not too much. You may even have well meaning, God fearing people telling you this, but this is not the truth.

When we come to Jesus we can get our hopes up because our hope is in what has Christ done for us. When we were still in sin Christ died for us, he rose again and has freed us from judgement and condemnation, now all things are working together for our good! The word tells us that "all the promises of God are yes in him." (2 Cor 1:20).

Our hope, then, is not the kind that blindfolds itself to reality. It's the kind that looks at a newly sealed tomb and says, "This story's not over."

We do not deny the circumstances that confront us, but we deny them a place of authority. Look to Jesus, look to the promises, and hold fast to them. Hope comes from the promises of God rooted in the work of Jesus. As 1 Peter 1:13 tells us *"set your hope fully on the grace that will be brought to you at the revelation of Jesus Christ"*

With that revelation of Jesus growing in us grace is brought to us. The more we see of Jesus, the more grace we will receive. We may at times experience sorrow, be burdened, broken, and beaten up, but we will not be a cynical people. We are a people of hope.

I would have lost heart, unless I had believed That I would see the goodness of the Lord In the land of the living. (Psalm 27:1).

11

Let Him Renew your soul

He makes me lie down in green pastures, he leads me beside quiet waters, he refreshes my soul.

Psalm 23:2-3

A re you someone who finds it easy to relax and unwind? In a fast paced world, where everyone seems to be constantly on the go we can forget what it means to take time out and ensure we are building in moments of solitude where we can be refreshed and recharged. The world will tell us to go for spa day, to treat ourselves to a night away or to play a round of golf! All these things are great but they can totally miss the point! We could be playing golf on the most beautiful course in the world, with the best golfers, be winning the game and yet still not find any rest. Your body can be in one place but your mind can be elsewhere.

Too often people are looking for an escape when they feel depleted and try to recharge physically and emotionally when they feel like their batteries are running down. We all need times when life slows down and we can get a change of scenery. But the Lord's refreshing is more than this. The Lord wants us to find a new way to live, a new pace in which we don't simply survive but we thrive.

You see rest is an inner state. It's the internal work that the Lord wants to do in us to ensure that we can live our lives to the full and experience the freedom that He died to bring us. So how can we walk in this place of peace where we find the stillness and refreshing for which our souls crave?

If we meditate on these verses we will begin to find some answers.

"He makes me lie down....." I don't know about you but I certainly don't get much done when I am lying down. When we think of lying down we associate it with sleeping and resting. Normally for us to sleep we need to be at peace, to have ceased all our effort and to have let go.

This is the internal posture that the Lord wants us to take when it comes to life. It's not that we live a life void of activity or productivity but he wants us to learn a rhythm of life that draws from his unlimited supply and not our own which soon runs out. In order for us to do this we need to create moments in our lives where we are no longer bombarded by demands but instead we become aware of his abundant supply.

"Green pastures.." speak to us of rich fertile land. A land that will produce everything that is needed to sustain life. The Lord wants our hearts to be overwhelmed by the fact that we are surrounded by his abundance and blessing. He wants us to rest in this land knowing that He has taken care of all the needs we have. In a dry land we will fear for our provision but a green land speaks of a place that is well watered receiving everything it needs to bear fruit.

"He leads me beside still waters...." Our worlds are full of voices. The physical voices of our bosses, kids, spouses, friends, family and even the media. But there are also the internal voices that we hear, the lies the enemy tries to tell us, our self doubt and insecurities. This is why the Lord wants to take us to a quiet place. A place where all of the voices are silenced and we listen to the one voice who brings life. The voice of truth, the voice that speaks a better promise. The voice that calls us to see ourselves as He sees us and the voice that calls us by name. Knowing everything about us and loving us perfectly and completely.

Today allow the Lord to lead you and set the pace for your life. As you follow the prompting of his Holy Spirit you will encounter him in ways that cause you to stop and pause. He will still you on the inside and you will be aware of his living water sustaining you and refreshing you. Renewing your soul and giving you hope for tomorrow!

12

Wait Expectantly

This is what the kingdom of God is like. A man scatters seed on the ground.
Night and day, whether he sleeps or gets up, the seed sprouts and grows,
though he does not know how."

Mark 4:26- 27

Are there things in life that baffle you? Things that you don't really understand? I would consider myself to be technologically challenged at times. When it comes to fixing IT problems I tend to rely on my son or my husband. There are things that I just don't properly understand but to be honest I don't need to know, as long as I can do emails, presentations and create documents I am happy in my ignorance.

As we become familiar and comfortable with things around us we learn to trust them. When we get on a plane we don't understand aeronautical engineering but we trust that the pilot knows what he is doing and that he will get us to our destination safely. When I went for a scan with my first baby I could not really make out all the organs and parts of my baby's body on the screen but I trusted the doctors knew what they were looking for and that my baby was healthy.

When it comes to the Lord's plans for our lives He wants us to learn to trust Him and to put our confidence in His word. Jesus shows us through today's parable how He wants us to approach the word and what actions he requires us to take. You see the word is the seed. When we declare it over our lives and come into agreement with the Lord's promises for us it is like putting the seed into the ground. Now the really interesting part is what comes next. Many of us understand that our role is to believe in the Lord's promises and to speak them into being. However where many of us struggle is with the next part.

What does the farmer do once he has sown his seed? *"Night and day, whether he sleeps or gets up, the seed sprouts and grows,"* The farmers activity is done once the seed is sown. At this point his work is complete, he doesn't need to add to it, we read whether he is sleeping or awake the seed sprouts and grows. Even more amazing is the fact that the farmer doesn't even know how it all works and he is not required to. Once he puts the seed into the ground he can go about his business confident that the harvest will come at the appointed time.

Jesus gives us this illustration to help us. To provide a clear picture for us. To teach us his way and to give us assurance about how his kingdom operates so that we can fully rely and depend on him. I know in my life that I often start off with great intentions, I take hold of God's promises with hope and expectation. I speak the word over my life with excitement and anticipation and then I wait eagerly to see the results. But as the days pass by and everything appears to have stayed the same, doubt begins to creep in and I begin to wonder whether I did my part the way I was supposed to.

Am I missing something? Did I get it wrong? Do I need to spend more time in prayer, study harder, behave better, have more faith? Is there somewhere I'm missing it? Have I not been obedient? Suddenly my thoughts are off the Lord and his work and I'm focusing on my work and what I have or haven't done and how this could be hindering the promises of God being fulfilled in my life.

Look again at today's verse: *"though he does not know how."* We don't need to know how the seed grows. We place it in the ground and the Lord does the rest. He wants us to go about our lives, getting on with what is in front of us. Enjoying Him, enjoying our families, friends, jobs, church. He wants us to have confidence that the seed is growing, independent of us. Even when it might look like nothing is happening the roots are sprouting and the work is taking place behind the scenes. At the right time we will see the sprouts breaking through. Wait expectantly, with hope in your heart, for these shoots to come through and praise Jesus, as He encourages you through the word, that your harvest is on the way.

13

Trust that He is working

All by itself the soil produces grain—first the stalk, then the head, then the full kernel in the head.

Mark 4:28

A re you someone who enjoys gardening? Although I love to look at colourful flowerbeds and I appreciate a well tended garden, I have to say that it is not something that comes naturally to me. I often dread being bought plants as presents because I then feel the pressure to keep them alive and feel guilty if the person who has given me the gift comes to visit and sees the wilting plant crying for help in the corner.

I do, however, love flowers and one particular plant that has managed to stay alive in my garden is the daffodil. When I moved into our house it was in the summer so it wasn't until the following spring that I got up one morning and noticed lots of green shoots starting to break through the soil in our over grown flower bed. Knowing that I hadn't planted anything I was delighted to find out that below the ground was a whole lot of bulbs that had been secretly growing and in a matter of weeks there was a sea of beautiful yellow flowers filling the garden with life and calling in the start of Spring.

This was a great lesson to me that highlighted today's verse. It didn't actually matter that I had no particular skill or knowledge about gardening. The bulb and the soil did what they were designed to do. They brought forth new life. What was incredible to me was that this life was being formed without me knowing anything about it. Someone else had planted the seed and I was getting to enjoy the fruit of it.

Today many of us are living in the blessing of words that have been spoken over our lives by others. We get to walk in goodness and blessing because people have declared favour, provision, health and wholeness over us. This encourages me and also inspires me about the words of life that I can sow into my life for myself and into the lives of those around me.

God has given us these pictures to build confidence in us when it comes to understanding how his kingdom works . He knows that we need to have a reference point as we learn to trust him and walk by faith so He gives us these images to hold onto. Today if you have believed the word in an area of your life, whether it be your finances, your health, your relationships, your future partner, your ministry or your career, have assurance that as you have spoken in faith and sown a seed the Lord is working below ground.

Even the process of how the plant grows is there to give us comfort and patience as we journey and depend on the Lord's timing. "First the blade...." How often do we see small indications of things starting to change? It could be positive feedback from your boss, a connection out of the blue, or a chance encounter with an old friend. Do you see these signs as the blade and praise God for the work that he is doing in your life?

There are times when we are too busy looking for the big thing to appear, for a voice from heaven. God doesn't normally operate in this way. You don't wake up one morning to see fully grown daffodils blowing about in the wind. They come gradually, day by day. Sometimes you hardly notice. If you were to sit and watch one all day it would probably seem like nothing is happening. But over time we see growth until the flower finally blooms and becomes everything it was created to be.

Notice there are stages to the development. Remember our verse : *The stalk, the head and the full kernel.* The Lord works out the plan for your life in steps. It doesn't come all at once. It doesn't happen over night. Most of the time you think that nothing is changing but trust that He is working, He is moving, the seeds you have sown are coming to life and you will reap a harvest!

14

Sow the word in your life

As soon as the grain is ripe, he puts the sickle to it, because the harvest has come.

Mark 4:29

Are you waking up today with confidence about your future? Are you expecting good things to happen in your life? Whatever you are feeling today you can be sure that God is preparing favour and blessing for you. Even if you can't see it at the minute or you can't quite believe that you deserve it He wants you to turn from your unbelief and begin to embrace the thoughts that He is thinking about your destiny.

There are many things that are uncertain in life. So much in our worlds have been shaken in recent times and many of the things that we have trusted in such as careers or routines have been turned upside down. Even our ability to have close fellowship with other believers had been made more difficult for a time. And yet in the midst of this upheaval as many things have been stripped away we have had the opportunity to see that there is one thing that is steadfast and sure.

The Lord is unchanging. His love towards us will never fail and He has proved his love to us through giving us his Son. Nothing has been held back from us. God gave us everything and this is why we can be assured today that *He who did not spare his own Son, but gave him up for us all—how will he not also, along with him, graciously give us all things?* (Romans 8:32).

Whatever situation we find ourselves in, whatever problems we may be facing we can know today that we are not alone. The Lord has not designed us to carry heavy burdens. He has not intended for us to make it in our own strength. He has given us the keys to succeed in life and he wants us to learn from him today about how we can access the riches of his kingdom and walk in the fullness of life that His son died to bring us.

So what are these keys? Well he wants us to trust in his power. To have confidence that his principles are sure and that we can put our faith in his word and see our lives being transformed by his love and grace.

The farmer when he goes out and plants the seed does so with certainty because his life literally depends on it. If he has no crops, he has no income and he will not survive. But the farmer sows with an assurance, knowing that as the seed goes into the ground it has everything that it needs to produce the grain. He doesn't overthink it, he doesn't second guess, he doesn't go and dig it up when he can't see anything changing. He waits for harvest time.

We all understand in the natural that farmers plant at one time in the year and then harvest at another. We don't ask them in the middle of the summer if the harvest is ready because we understand this is foolishness.

But just because we can't see the full fruit we don't doubt that the harvest will be good.

Believe today that God has made the way for you to receive the abundance of his grace in your life. Know that there is nothing that He is holding back from you. Through Christ today you can expect to inherit "all things."

How much clearer can the Lord make it for us. It's health, wholeness, freedom from fear, peace, completeness, prosperity, soundness of mind. Everything that you feel you need today the Lord has already graciously supplied through Jesus. So sow the word in your life, come into agreement with what the Lord has poured out upon you and be excited for the harvest that will come!!

15

Jesus has set you free!

He has taken your guilt and shame. Look, nothing deserving death has been done by him.

Luke 23:15

There are not many of us who can put our hands on our hearts and say I hardly ever make a mistake or get it wrong. I think most of us in the course of a day will have times when we wished we hadn't said, thought or acted in a certain way. I don't say this to condemn anyone as we know that thanks to the blood of Jesus the Lord is not looking at our imperfections. He is not focused on what we get wrong, he chooses to see us through the lens of his son who is the one perfect man.

We understand that when it comes to Jesus, however, there is a standard that is beyond human striving and performance. He came to earth and revealed to us that His ways are above our own. Where we might strive to be more loving or caring, He is in his nature love and compassion. He doesn't try to be something, He simply is!

That is why we know that whenever people encountered Jesus it was obvious that He was a pure and innocent man. As Jesus was brought before Pilate by the Jewish authorities and the angry crowd there was no charge that he could find against him. He was guiltless. In this passage Luke the author really wants us to take note of this - Three times in Luke 23:15-22 Pilate declares Jesus' innocence. First, in verse 15, he says, "Look, nothing deserving death has been done by him." Second, in verse 20, Luke tell us, "Pilate addressed them once more, desiring to release Jesus..." Then, in verse 22, Luke says, "A third time [Pilate] said to them, 'Why, what evil has he done? I have found in him no guilt deserving death.'"

Three times in this short span of eight verses, Luke, through Pilate, points us to Jesus' innocence. Jesus has done nothing deserving of death. He is innocent. Then later in the chapter, the theme of Jesus' innocence will be echoed again, by both the thief on the cross and by the centurion. The thief on the cross will say to the other thief in verse 41, "We are receiving the due reward of our deeds; but this man has done nothing wrong." And the centurion will say at Jesus' death in verse 47: "Certainly this man was innocent!"

Luke shows us at least six clear declarations of Jesus' innocence in this chapter. Pilate initially found no guilt in Jesus, then neither did Herod, after this Pilate declares Jesus' innocence three more times, and finally not only the thief on the cross but also the centurion affirm this. We can be of no doubt to the truth of Jesus' position in this trial and yet we see how Pilate, rather than following his instincts and what is clearly just, chooses instead to appease the crowd.

What would appear to be the greatest act of injustice by man, God turns into the greatest moment in human history, where his divine justice is

44

poured out for all mankind for all eternity.

Today we can have confidence in the fact that the God of justice and mercy has wiped the slate clean. He came as the innocent one and took our penalty, so that today we can receive his forgiveness, favour and blessings on our lives. We get to go guilt free. No matter what situation you may come against, what voice may rise up and call you guilty, know today that you can have hope because Jesus the perfectly innocent one has set you free.

16

Jesus has already responded in love towards you

But they all cried out together, "Away with this man, and release to us Barabbas.

Luke 23:18-19

Are there times when you have dared to stand out from the crowd? To hold your position and go against the grain is no easy feat. Much research has been done on the influence of the crowd and how often we adopt a herd mentality based largely on emotional, rather than rational thinking. It can have a devastating effect and people can find themselves making choices that they would never normally have contemplated. We have seen instances throughout history of unthinkable atrocities, within the last 40 years we saw genocide sweep the nation of Rwanda as the madness of the crowd reigned.

When Jesus walked the earth He understood the weakness of human nature and He was not surprised by the actions of the crowd. In John 2:24-25 we read "*But Jesus would not entrust himself to them, for he knew all people. He did not need any testimony about mankind, for he knew what was in each person."*

In today's passage it is easy to read it and feel outraged at what is taking place, particularly when we are introduced to the character of Barabbas. His life intersects the story at the trial of Jesus. Mark 15:6 tells us that the release of a Jewish prisoner was customary before the feast of Passover. The Roman governor would have granted a pardon to one criminal as an act of goodwill towards the Jews whom he governed. The choice Pilate set before them could not have been more clear-cut: a high-profile killer and rabble-rouser who was unquestionably guilty, or a teacher and miracle-worker who was demonstrably innocent.

Everyone knows that Barabbas is the guilty one here. Just after Pilate has said, "Look, nothing deserving death has been done by him," Luke tells us in verses 18–19, *"But they all cried out together, 'Away with this man, and release to us Barabbas."* What is happening? How could they possibly prefer to see this man walk free. This is a man who had been thrown into prison for an insurrection started in the city and for murder. It is Barabbas who is the guilty, says Luke. He is the same man called "a notorious prisoner" in Matthew 27:16, and Mark tells us that Barabbas was "among the rebels in prison, who had committed murder in the insurrection."

We are appalled at their suggestions, we are outraged by the injustice. Barrabas is clearly the guilty one who deserves to pay for the crimes he has committed. But what we fail to see is that the freedom granted to Barrabas is the same freedom that we get to walk in today because as Barrabas walks free another man who is guiltless pays the price with his life.

Let's look again at his name. I love the significance in all the details. BAR means "The son of," "ABBA " the Father." Now let's piece all this together and see what the Lord is revealing to us. The son of Abba .....Barrabas is guilty of rebellion and murder. Who does Barrabas represent? He represents each one of us. We have been created in the image of God, we are his own offspring and we have rebelled against Him. Barrabas sits on death row waiting to be sentenced to death for the sin He has committed and his maker steps out of heaven to set him free. He is the substitute. He is the innocent one.

Suddenly with fresh eyes I realise my view of Barrabas is changing. He is no longer the horrendous villain in the story. He is the picture of fallen humanity, held captive by our own evil choices and in need of a saviour. God loves Barrabas, just like God loves me and is willing to surrender everything so that I can find life today. Take comfort that no matter how far you think you have fallen, or how big a mess or terrible a choice you could make, Jesus has already responded in love towards you. You can live full of hope today because the God of all hope has made a way out for you.

"But God shows his love for us in that while we were still sinners, Christ died for us." (Romans 5:8).

17

Don't be anxious over the future

So Pilate decided that their demand should be granted. He released the man who had been thrown into prison for insurrection and murder, for whom they asked, but he delivered Jesus over to their will.

Luke 23:24-25

Are there times when you can't see a way out? Have you had days when it feels like it is all coming crashing down around you? Maybe it's the break up of a relationship, perhaps you have had a bad report from the doctor or you might have had someone slander you. We all have moments when life can feel out of our control. There are times the mess can be of our own making and others when circumstances or people have just come against us. Whatever the case, I want to encourage you today that there is one who is above it all and who is working on your behalf.

We read today of Pilate's part in Jesus' death. How a man of authority, who could clearly see that Jesus was innocent, chose not to follow his better judgement but allowed himself to be swayed by the crowd. As people we are frail and weak. We often allow fear to dictate our actions and we can be intimidated by the pressure of what others will think or do. Pilate for all the position and power that he held, was still unable to stand for what he believed to be right. He considered his own reputation more important than delivering justice.

There may be days when you are on the other end of someone's failure to show leadership and act with integrity. There may be times when people fail to speak up for you and come to your defense. You might think that your rights are being sacrificed in order for someone to guarantee their own career advancement. You might find that no one is willing to stand in faith with you and believe for healing in case they are charged with giving you a false sense of hope in the face of the facts.

I want to encourage you today that whatever plans the enemy might have, whatever weakness we see in the flesh, we need not despair. The Lord's plans and purposes are not thwarted by the schemes of man. When I examine these verses I love to ponder the words and phrases and see how the Lord shows me his bigger plan. It says " he (Pilate) delivered Jesus over to their will." Many of us need to recognise whose will is ultimately at play in our lives. No matter how many plans the religious authorities made, how many people were coerced, how much deception went on behind the scenes, nothing stood in the way of what the Lord had ordained from the foundation of the earth.

When it comes to the future we need to recognise that the Lord knows the end from the beginning. (Isaiah 46:10) There is nothing up ahead that will shock him or take him by surprise. Often in the very moment the enemy believes he has finally snuffed out your hopes, dreams, future and at times your very life, the exact opposite is happening.

The religious leaders finally believed they would put an end to their problems once and for all. They had manipulated the crowd, they had pressurised those in power, they had pulled strings and plotted evil and Jesus' day of reckoning had finally come. No longer would their system be challenged. Life would go back to the way that it was and after making a spectacle of Jesus no one would dare to oppose them again.

Yet as Jesus was delivered into their hands they didn't realise that they were actually walking Jesus to his destiny. They were helping him accomplish his mission on earth. As their anger and hatred is poured out on Jesus He absorbs all the evil that man can muster and allows it to consume his life. When their will is executed as he dies on the cross we see that the ultimate will of the Father is accomplished as death and separation are defeated. Jesus makes a way for us to be freed from the power of sin and to walk into the light of his love.

Jesus actually provides a way for the ones who are responsible for his death to find life, hope and a future. He surrenders his will to the Father and in doing so enters into his rightful place of honour and glory as our King forever.

Don't fear the plans that are made against you. Don't be anxious over the future. The Lord's plan for your life is for blessing, wholeness, peace and joy. He has already defeated every evil work. Live free today with hope in your heart and trust his will.

18

He declares you worthy

"All have sinned and fall short of the glory of God."

Romans 3:23

As a parent I often find myself playing the role of referee. As much we try and get our kids to work things out themselves, you can guarantee there are times when all sense of reason breaks down and we are called to step in before any serious damage is done!!

Whatever age we are, we all have this in built sense of justice and we all want to be treated fairly. We want others to pay for what they have done wrong and conversely, when it comes to ourselves we want people to show us grace and make allowances for our mistakes.

When it comes to approaching the Lord one of the greatest and most humbling things is the fact that we are all on an even keel. No matter how good we might think we are compared to another, none of us will ever be able to match up to the perfect standard of the law. We might put on a mask for others and try to appear like we have it all together but deep down we can't kid ourselves. We know when we lie and don't tell the full story. We know when we could have lent a hand but we made excuses as to why we were too busy. We know when we fail to speak up for what's right.

What we need to remember today is the fact that the Lord knows all of this too and more importantly it doesn't change the way that He feels about us. When we come to him in humility with all our weaknesses and failures and tell him that we need his help, he steps right in and reminds us of his love, forgiveness and grace.

I think many people today are struggling in life because they are living with this internal tension. They want to be someone that they are not. They long to be more loving, more patient, a better Mum, Dad, husband, daughter or friend. They have a picture in their minds of what that should look like and they compare themselves with others who they presume are doing a much better job.

What I love about today's verse is that no matter how great or awful you might think you are in Jesus' eyes he sees us all the same. We were lost sheep and He is our shepherd. He loves us and calls us by name. We belong to him. Whether we think we're the black sheep of the family or the favourite child it makes no difference in Jesus' eyes. We all have fallen short. We all need a saviour and Jesus loves to come and rescue us.

The incredible thing about the Lord's grace is that He not only rescues us from what we deserve but He freely gives us what we don't deserve. All this week we have been looking at the character of Barrabas. At first we see him as the guilty one, but then we recognise that he actually represents us all. Man who has rebelled against God. We know from

Romans 6:23 that *"the wages of sin is death."* But what is the Lord's response towards us? Pilate releases Barabbas the guilty, and delivers over to death Jesus the innocent. This is the picture of the Lord's love in action towards us today. In Barabbas we have a glimpse of our guilt deserving death, and a preview of the arresting grace of Jesus and his embrace of the cross through which we are set free.

This demonstration of love is so scandalous. Jesus became our substitute. Imagine yourself today standing on that platform as Jesus walks towards the cross. He says I will go for you so that you live free. You could never do it so I will do it for you. Your guilt is without question but I go in your place. It seems so unfair and so unjust. What can I do? What can I add? .....Nothing.......The only way in which we can respond is to believe and receive.

The greatest lesson we can learn today is that He is enough. You don't need to try harder to become someone today you just need to understand who you have become in Him. You are favoured, blessed and fully acceptable to God. As you draw close to Jesus, your saviour and magnify His work in your life you will no longer live with that internal tension that asks, "Am I good enough?" He has declared you enough today because you are no longer part of this world of comparison, competition and performance. Instead you are part of his heavenly kingdom and He declares you worthy.

19

Boldness for your future

"For the wages of sin is death, but the free gift of God is eternal life in Christ Jesus our Lord."

Romans 6:23

Most of us have a more than conceptual understanding of the term wages. We work and as a result we receive what we deserve. My son used to waste his pocket money on online games buying virtual outfits for characters. It was only when he began to earn the money for himself that he had a different perspective towards it. Suddenly the £10 that he had earned from 2 hours of painting the fence had more value than before. It had cost him something. He had put in time and effort. Before he spent this he wanted to consider how he could get the most out of it.

When it comes to our spiritual lives we also have a built in radar, our conscience, that reminds us of what we deserve based upon our actions. The wages that we can expect from our sin, the Bible tells us clearly are death. This may sound harsh and it is where our understanding of the term sin needs to be expanded. When Paul writes the wages of sin is death. He uses the greek word "*harmartia.*" This word is actually a noun and is referring to our sinful nature that we were born with. It is not referring to the separate acts of sin that we might commit each day.

Death comes from living outside of the fullness of God. When we choose to walk away from Jesus and find our own way in life, we walk away from the light of his love and find ourselves stumbling in the dark. If there's hopelessness, despair, anxiety or heaviness know today this is not the Lord's plan for you. He has come to set you free from sin and bondage, He wants you to experience your true life in Him.

There is no life outside of a life with Jesus. Many people might be existing but they are not experiencing the abundant life that they were created for. The Lord did not create us just to survive and get by in life but we were created to thrive!

The free gift of eternal life that this verse speaks of, is available to you today. Many times we look at our failings and weaknesses and we discount ourselves. We feel like we don't deserve it. Even as believers there are times when we mess up and let ourselves down and in these moments we often find that we turn away from the Lord because we don't believe we can receive from him. Our conscience is telling us what our sins deserve and we look away from the Lord in shame not believing we are worthy to be called his child, even less be treated as one.

What we need to remind ourselves of everyday is the truth of this scripture. "*The free gift of God.*" We were never good enough to receive it in the first place. There was nothing we could have done to earn it. It was never based on our performance or behaviour, it was only ever based on his love for us. We did not receive because we were worthy, we received because He is worthy.

This life eternal is not simply a life that will begin the day that we breathe our last breath on this earth. This life starts now. John 17: 3 tells us *"Now this is eternal life: that they know you, the only true God, and Jesus Christ, whom you have sent."* When we draw close to the Lord and allow his presence to fill our lives we will know his peace, joy, goodness and love filling our days. What's more we will have hope, assurance, confidence and boldness for our future.

20

No longer a slave

"In speaking of a new covenant, he makes the first one obsolete. And what is becoming obsolete and growing old is ready to vanish away"

Hebrews 8:13

When I was training to be a coach, one of the key behaviours I needed to be aware of was ensuring I adopted a non-judgemental attitude. I was challenged to think over every coaching conversation and reflect on how I had come across to the client.

Judgement is defined as "an opinion or decision that is based on careful thought." It can have serious implications on how we view ourselves and how we relate to others. People who feel judged describe feeling isolated, ashamed, misunderstood, criticised and demeaned. Judging can also result in people being less likely to talk about what they're going through and ask for the help they need. Judgment does not free us from our sin and our habits but in fact it strengthens them. It reinforces the deepest root in our lives - condemnation.

The greatest need that we have is to be free from condemnation. *Katakrima* is the Greek word for condemnation, meaning that we deserve the penalty once we have been judged. This is often the conclusion that we come to about ourselves. We end up with an opinion or decision that is based on careful thought when we think about what we do or have done on any particular day. It reinforces that root which is condemnation, if we believe we are guilty then we can't shake off the belief that a price must be paid. Punishment must be served for our behaviour.

When there's condemnation, there will be fear. We will always be afraid that our actions are not enough. Whatever price we pay we are still left feeling that the debt is not totally cancelled. This nagging fear will lead to stress as we live with turmoil on the inside. And when there's stress, there will be manifestations of the curse.

When we are under judgement there can be no hope or faith because we remain under the weight of a price that we owe but can never pay. Many of us are hearing the promise of freedom that grace brings but we find it hard to break free from the condemnation that grips us. Many of us still have a law problem even though we are under grace.

You may ask -What has the law got to do with my problems?

The devil is smarter than many psychiatrists, psychologists and even many believers. He does not deal with the peripherals and the superficial. His first name is not "thief" or "murderer", even though he steals and murders. His first name is Satan, which is Hebrew for "prosecutor of law" or "accuser" Think about the role of a prosecutor in a court of law. He is there to condemn you. He never talks about your good points. He will bring up all the dirty laundry and relentlessly accuses you till you feel condemned. He comes to say things like, "Call yourself a Christian!'

'Call yourself a good father. You're a lousy father!" He accuses you till you feel unworthy. and he uses the law, which is holy, good and just, to condemn you.

That is why condemnation—the root cause of all your problems—is so subtle. It can easily go undetected because when you look at yourself in your own estimation you know that what the accuser says is true. You alone are not worthy. But that is the whole reason why we need a loving saviour to lift us out of our sin and destruction and to set us free.

*"But when the fullness of time had come, God sent forth his Son, born of woman, born under the law, to **redeem those who were under the law, so that we might receive adoption as sons.** And because you are sons, God has sent the Spirit of his Son into our hearts, crying, "Abba! Father!" So you are **no longer a slave, but a son,** and if a son, then an heir through God"* (Galatians 4:4-7).

Meditate on this today, you are no longer a slave you have been redeemed from this life of bondage and death. You have been brought into a new family where the Father lavishes his love on you. He is not judging you based on what you do, he is loving you based on who you are, His precious child.

21

You are His Beloved

You do not know what manner of spirit you are of. For the Son of Man did not come to destroy men's lives but to save them."

Luke 9:54–56

Do you live each day conscious of your mistakes or your right standing with Jesus? Many Christians struggle to draw close to the Lord when they fail because they still believe that God is judging them when they mess up or behave badly. I know in my own life I could be preparing a talk or arranging something for church. Next minute I am interrupted by a mini drama with my kids fighting over goodness knows what! Despite my best efforts I end up losing my temper. When all the dust settles and I turn back to writing about the Word and encouraging people, suddenly I feel worthless. "What do I have to offer? How could I possibly give encouragement and guidance from the word when I am such a failure?"

That's the voice that I battle with in my mind! Does it sound familiar? That accusation that leaves you feeling hopeless and useless. As believers we need to make sure that we are really taking hold of the truth of God's word. In Christ we will no longer be judged for our wrongdoing. Listen to me very clearly - Under the law, judgement is always greater than the sacrifice. But under grace, the sacrifice is always greater than judgement. Let me show you one of the stories that has kept believers locked into a mindset that there is still judgement.

There is a story in the Old testament of a literal fire judgment that fell upon the enemies of the prophet Elijah. It is told in 2 Kings 1:1–15 and there are other accounts of God's judgment such as upon Sodom and Gomorrah (Gen. 19:24–25). But God wants us to be able to rightly divide His Word (2 Tim. 2:15). He wants us to be astute in rightly dividing and clearly separating what belongs to the old covenant of law and what belongs to the new covenant of grace. We need to be able to distinguish what occurred before the cross from what occurred after the cross and to understand the difference the cross has made. Many believers today are living as if the cross did not make any difference at all!

Don't just take it from me that God will not call down the fires of judgment on you today. See for yourself what Jesus said about what Elijah did. Do you remember the time when Jesus wanted to enter a certain village in Samaria, but the people there refused to receive Him? When Jesus' disciples saw that the people rejected Jesus, they said, *"Lord, do You want us to command fire to come down from heaven and consume them, just as Elijah did?"* Now, how did Jesus respond to them? Did He say, "That's a great idea! You are truly disciples who carry My heart"? No, of course not! Read your Bible. He turned to His disciples and rebuked them firmly, saying, *"You do not know what manner of spirit you are of. For the Son of Man did not come to destroy men's lives but to save them"* (Luke 9:54–56).

This is the Lord's heart for us today. To save us, to rescue us out of sin and death and to redeem us. To lift us out of bondage and to lead us into a life of freedom and blessing.

For by one offering He has perfected forever those who are being sanctified. (Hebrews 10:12-14).

Your salvation is not based on a feeling, it is based on a fact. Jesus took your penalty and died in your place. You no longer get what you deserve, you get what He deserves. The perfect one has perfected us forever. It was a one time act that will last for eternity. What heaven has declared finished man can not undo. Moreover know that He is working out his purposes in our lives, as we are being sanctified. The amplified version explains more fully what that means. He is *"bringing each believer to spiritual completion and maturity."* He is helping you overcome all the things that can hinder and ensnare you. He is working salvation in you everyday to help you see and become all that He has created you to be. He doesn't judge. He speaks love towards you today and declares you, his beloved accepted and righteous!

22

Walk Freely

Blessed is the one whose transgressions are forgiven, whose sins are covered. Blessed is the one whose sin the Lord does not count against them and in whose spirit is no deceit.

Psalm 32:1-2

When it comes to our everyday life we can take comfort in the fact that the Lord is interested in it all. It is not simply the spiritual aspects of our lives that the Lord is invested in. In Phil 4:19 Paul writes that *my God shall supply all your need according to His riches in glory by Christ Jesus.*

All your needs, - that means every single one - physical, emotional, spiritual were all met through the work of the cross. God does not provide multiple solutions for the many different problems facing us today. He is not like a phone system when we hear "Press button 1 to receive help in this area." Jesus will reach out to heal, restore, deliver and provide. But what holds many of us back is the thought that we are unworthy. How can we have confidence that we are good enough to deserve his blessings? Can we really accept the fact that our sins have been forgiven?

The Bible tells us that an ALL sufficient sacrifice has been made through Jesus. His sacrifice is enough. *"Christ has redeemed us from the curse of the law, having become a curse for us for it is written, 'Cursed is everyone who hangs on a tree' that the blessing of Abraham might come upon the Gentiles in Christ Jesus."* (Gal 3:13-14).

So when it comes to our sin, how does the Lord judge us? This is a question that many of us grapple with and in order for us to walk in freedom we need to assure our hearts with evidence from the word. In what way does he look at us and how does he view our sins?

The Father has been revealing his heart of mercy towards us throughout scripture. We read in the psalms of the revelation he gave to David regarding his sin and failure. David was a man who was aware of his own weakness and many times humbled himself before the Lord when we was confronted with his frailty and mess. In today's verses from Psalm 32 we read how David sought and received God's forgiveness. The Hebrew word for forgiven here literally means "lifted off." Isn't this beautiful? This is how the Lord wants you to feel when you come before him with a humble heart and tell him your need of him. You see, unconfessed sin is a burden that weighs us down. When we confess our sin to God, He lifts it off our shoulders, rolls it away, and it disappears. He wants us to walk freely today knowing that there is nothing held against us.

Ps. 32:1 and Rom. 4:7 also tell us that "He covers our sin." This imagery is taken from the Day of Atonement. On this day the high priest took blood from a sacrificial animal, carried it into the Most Holy Place, and sprinkled it on the mercy seat of the ark of the covenant (a chest that contained the Ten Commandments). The sprinkled blood symbolically covered the broken law and shielded the sinner from judgment. It's significant that when David stopped trying to cover up his sin (v. 5), God "covered" it (v. 1).

When something is covered, it's hidden from view. God puts our sin out of His sight. How many of us are living with this revelation today that God has not only dealt with our sin but it has been put away from His view. We often allow our past mistakes to play on repeat in our minds. We live today with our thoughts stuck in the past, beating ourselves up about what we should have done and torturing ourselves with regrets. The Lord wants us to be set free from this bondage. We are a new creation in him and each day we receive grace and mercy.

Furthermore as we read on in Psalm 32 we see that *He does not charge us with iniquity.* "Charge" is a bookkeeping term which he uses to show us that He no longer counts our sin against us. This same imagery is used by Paul in Romans 4. God charges our sin to Jesus' ledger (who bore our penalty) and writes Jesus' righteousness into our ledger and credits us with His righteousness (Rom. 4:8-25).

How much clearer can the Lord make it for us. We are forgiven, the weight is lifted off us, our sins are covered and out of sight and there is no charge against us, in fact we are credited with His righteousness.

Meditate on these truths today and allow them to bring life, freedom and hope to your heart!

23

Your stain is gone

"I, even I, am he who blots out your transgressions, for my own sake, and remembers your sins no more."

Isaiah 43:25

How many of you remember blotting paper and what it was used for? For those not old enough to recall, blotting paper was a thick absorbent paper that was used when writing with a fountain pen. The fountain pen made your handwriting take on a beautiful calligraphy style as the wet water-based ink flowed from the metal nib of the fountain pen. Blotting paper was used to absorb the excess liquid ink after writing. If you didn't use blotting paper before you closed your writing pad the wet ink would stain the opposite page. The blotting paper 'took away' the ability of the wet ink to stain what it touched.

Isaiah 1:18 says *"You are stained red with sin, but I will wash you as clean as snow. Although your stains are deep red, you will be as white as wool."* As a spilled glass of red wine will stain everything it comes into contact with, we have all experienced the stain of sin in our lives. But this verse is not focused on our sin, it's focused on the promise that our red stain of sin would become as white as snow. This was a promise of what Jesus would accomplish at the cross when He exchanged His righteousness for our sin.

In the Old Testament, the same sacrifices had to be made every year because animal sacrifices made by humans can never 'take away' the stain of sin. This annual atonement only acted as a 'cover-up.' In the same way a lovely white tablecloth can cover the stain on your wooden kitchen table, but it can never take it away, the stain is still there underneath – and you know it's there!

When John the Baptist saw Jesus coming towards him he didn't declare "here comes the Lamb of God who will 'cover-up' the sins of the world." No, he says "Behold! The Lamb of God who 'takes away' the sin of the world!" (John 1:29). The sacrifice of Jesus finished all sacrifices, the sin of mankind was completely forgiven and forgotten. God is not holding your sin against you (2 Corinthians 5:19).

That's why God can say "For I will forgive their iniquities and will remember their sins no more." (Hebrews 8:12). God doesn't have a memory problem, He chooses to forget. As far as the east is from the west, so far has he removed our transgressions from us (Psalm 103:12), and from His memory. The Hebrew meaning for 'blots out' includes to obliterate and exterminate. Take a moment to think about that... your sin has been obliterated and exterminated from God's memory!

Thinking about our sin causes us to spiral down into guilt, shame, failure, defeat and bondage. If God's not holding your sin against you, then why would you? If God doesn't remember your wrongdoing, then why would you? God sees you as completely righteous through the sacrifice of Jesus on the cross - your stain is gone!

So today, choose to focus on your righteous position in Christ, rather than your failures, and this will cause you to rise up and walk with confidence and victory, knowing that you are a world overcomer, more than a conqueror and always triumphant in the face of every challenging situation.

24

The Price has been Paid

"having wiped out the handwriting of requirements that was against us, which was contrary to us. And He has taken it out of the way, having nailed it to the cross."

Colossians 2:14

The story is told of a woman who had an encounter with Jesus in a vision. Her pastor was continually troubled by something that he had done in his past. As the woman was a very credible lady, the pastor spoke with her about the vision and asked her if it happened again to ask Jesus about a thing which had troubled him from his past. Sure enough, after some time the woman had another encounter with Jesus. When the pastor found out he asked the woman if she had asked Jesus about this thing in his past. She replied that she had, and that Jesus had no idea what he was talking about!

How often do we torment and limit ourselves because of our failings, even though there is no record of them in the mind of God?

Jesus has wiped out the *handwriting of requirements* that were against us. *The handwriting of requirements* is the Old Testament law. This law was written by the very hand of God on tablets of stone. God also used Moses to write the fuller version of the law, known as the Torah, which is the first five books of the Bible. This law required perfection from imperfect people who couldn't meet the requirements of the law, but when Jesus went to the cross He wiped out the Old Testament law in its entirety. It's unfortunate that some still preach the law today even though Jesus wiped out its requirements at the cross.

The law was against us. It declared a standard we could not reach. It was contrary to us, it condemned us, it accused us, bringing only guilt and shame when we messed up and were unable to achieve God's standard of perfection. The law stood as a legal charge against us, a debt we owed but could not pay. However, Jesus, as a perfect man, was able to pay the price on our behalf.

Jesus wiped out our sin at the cross, becoming sin for us that we would become the righteousness of God (2 Corinthians 5:21). If that wasn't enough, He actually wiped out the law, taking it away and nailing it to the cross. It was the law that made us aware of our sin (Romans 3:20), for where there is no law there is no transgression (Romans 4:15) and where there is no law sin is not taken into account (Romans 5:13).

Right now, God is not counting our sins against us because Jesus wiped out the requirements of the law. The legal charge against us has been settled at the cross, it's been paid in full. Unlike an invoice that we owe, God doesn't just stamp "PAID" on it and then keep it for His records. No! The legal charge against us ceased to exist when it was wiped out and taken away, there is no longer a record of our debt, or our sin.

Today, there is no need to torment or limit ourselves because of our failings. There is no record of our failings in the mind of God. There is no need to assess ourselves from a performance perspective against God's law. Jesus has wiped out the law and its requirements. The price has been paid. Our sin, and the subsequent debt we owed has been removed from existence forever. Today, we can have hope for our future because the truth is: we are totally forgiven, completely righteous and made perfect by Jesus.

25

The Power of a Name

But now, this is what the Lord says— he who created you, Jacob, he who formed you, Israel: "Do not fear, for I have redeemed you; I have summoned you by name; you are mine.

Isaiah 43: 1

Names in bible times were very important. They were not just a way for people to identify each other but they actually had meaning and significance and spoke into the destiny of the person. If we look at the first man God created, He was named Adam. We are so familiar with the name now that we often don't take the time to think about its' meaning. Adam is derived from the Hebrew word *Adamah* meaning 'ground'. Adam was formed "from the dust of the ground" and so, his name (and the general Hebrew name for 'man') is rooted in how mankind began.

In today's passage we see how the Lord refers to his chosen people using the names Jacob and Israel. Here we see him reminding his people once more of his purpose and plans for their lives and his hand to save. We know from the book of Genesis that Jacob tricked his elder brother, lied to his father and stole his birthright. He lived into his name of *supplanter* or one who undermines. It was only after Jacob struggled with God and came to a place of surrender that he was given the name Israel, meaning "May God prevail." The Lord redeemed Jacob and changed his name. He took this man who had betrayed his family and he turned him into the Father of a great nation. God changed his identity from a supplanter to one who sees the Lord prevailing in his life and the lives of the generations to come.

Today we don't need to fear the future because our identity is in Christ. We too have been redeemed. Despite our failings or our past mistakes. Despite the struggles we have had and the times we have wrestled with the Lord. Despite the lies that we have believed and our unbelief, the Lord calls us his own. We belong to the one who created it all. Like Adam we have been formed by our loving heavenly Father. He has shaped us, fashioned us into being and he has called each one of us by name. This is the foundation of our faith. We belong to Jesus, the King of all kings.

So why do we become so intimidated by such small stuff? Why do we become overwhelmed by situations? The answer is simple: we lose sight of whose we are and all that that means.

Remember the children of Israel and how they wandered in the wilderness for forty years! We often think the Lord was just punishing them but he actually needed to let a whole generation die and their unbelief die with them. Fear held them back. Even though they were physically freed from slavery they still had the mindset of a slave. They could not see themselves as God's chosen people who were walking in his power and strength.

74

How do you see yourself today? Do you stop and meditate on who the Lord says you are and what that means or do you allow circumstance to overwhelm you?

The Lord wants to build our faith in him. He wants us to have confidence. The problem is we all like certainty and assurance. We all want to know the answers and know what's coming up ahead. But God has called us to walk by faith and not by sight. He wants to lead and guide us. For many of us if we knew what was ahead we would give up! If we could see all the obstacles and the hurdles we would run a mile because we would not believe we would have the courage to get through. Too often we approach situations from a natural perspective rather than a super natural perspective. We look to our natural abilities and we discount ourselves because we can't see how we can make it through.

The Lord wants us to approach things with boldness because of the living hope we have on the inside of us. He wants to move forward in the light of his power. He is training us to respond with eyes of faith and this will increase as we understand our true identity in Him.

26

He is preparing you for victory and success

When you pass through the waters, I will be with you; and when you pass through the rivers, they will not sweep over you. When you walk through the fire, you will not be burned; the flames will not set you ablaze.

Isaiah 43:2

Many times in life we feel overwhelmed. We think it's either sink or swim! Too often we are unable to imagine we have the strength to swim and we picture ourselves drowning in the circumstances. The media is talking a lot about the subject of mental health. People feeling unable to cope. This is one of the schemes of the devil, he tries to overwhelm us. Often he doesn't try to do it through one major event. Instead there are lots of little things that crowd in on us until we feel unable to breathe.

Why does he use this tactic? If it was just one thing we find a strategy to cope with it. When there are multiple sources of distraction and difficulty we feel overcome. The devil wants us to feel surrounded. So that we'll give up. But look again at today's verses: we *pass **through** the waters...*

. *And .... pass* **through** *the rivers......* We can have hope today because the trials we face are only ever temporary.

Look at the picture of the fire, here the scripture promises that we will walk through and we shall not be burned, the flames will not set you ablaze. We are not only promised that we will be able to make it through, but we will get through unharmed. We see this is literally proved to us in Daniel 3 with Shadrach, Meshach and Abednego when they are taken into captivity in Babylon . They are thrown into the fire by King Nebuchadnezzar but the Lord preserves them. They are protected by the presence of the Lord. That same protection is available to us today.

Notice every word in these verses gives us greater insight into the Lord's love and care for us. It says we will walk through the fire, not run. We don't need to be concerned or alarmed or panicked. When we walk we are not in a hurry. It's a picture of trust.

We are in the world but not off the world so we have a greater wisdom that flows from the Father. Many people are trying to find a way to persevere through trials and challenges and to conquer fear. In the business world people are now taught about how to be mentally tough. And research has highlighted that there are four key components to being able to grow in this area. They are the 4 C's : Confidence, Commitment, Challenge and Control. If we have to focus on these areas in our own strength that can become tiring but as believers we do not need to look to ourselves to be mentally tough!

We are confident, not in our ability but we have Confidence in who the Lord is and what he can do. When it comes to Commitment, we know that He is committed 100% to us and He will never give up on us. In terms of Control, we have an assurance that He is in control and because of that we have peace about whatever situations we may be facing. And for Challenge we know that the Lord will always work everything together for our good.

Today as believers we can be mentally tough! We can face life with courage and boldness not because we have learned to grit our teeth and get through but because the Lord has placed resurrection power on the inside of us. Jesus is our living hope. He is alive today and his life is flowing through us.

So know today that you can have confidence and hope because any trial you face is only temporary and the Lord will bring you through and moreover as we pass through these various trials and tribulations in life he is actually strengthening us. He is preparing us for greater levels of victory and success.

27

He will never leave you!

Do not be afraid, for I am with you; I will bring your children from the east and gather you from the west. I will say to the north, 'Give them up!' and to the south, 'Do not hold them back.' Bring my sons from afar and my daughters from the ends of the earth

Isaiah 43:5-6

We all have times in life when we feel anxious or worried about our future. It may be a difficult relationship, it could be a health issue or we may be struggling with our finances. Whatever the source we can find ourselves surrounded by fears and doubts about how we will make it through. Often what can become most frustrating is when people just tell us not to worry but they don't give an alternative for us to focus on.

This is why the word is so powerful. Many people hear about meditating on the word but feel that is something they are inexperienced in or that it is a skill they have not yet acquired. The reality is anyone and everyone can do it. If you have learnt how to worry you already know how to meditate! Now you just need to start channeling it in a new direction!

When we worry we overthink all the negative consequences that could possibly occur in our futures. When we meditate we simply think of the goodness of God and the truth of his word. Whenever the Lord tells us not to be afraid he gives us a reason why. Look in today's verses " Do not be afraid, for I am with you." We don't need to be fearful because we are not left to navigate our way through this life alone. We have the Lord leading us, guiding us and protecting us. Furthermore we see how He is always active on our behalf. His promises are not weak and vague. They are certain and sure. Look at the language he uses, he repeats the statements "I will," to the children of Israel, he promises affirmative action to lift them from their trials and to restore to them everything they have lost.

When we consider the context of this passage we recognise that this is the Lord's promise to his people in the face of their rejection and rebellion. Even when they are unfaithful and break their promises to the Lord He continues to prove himself faithful and just. As the Psalms tell us *The LORD is gracious and merciful; Slow to anger and great in loving kindness.* 145 :8 The Lord is always going ahead of you to provide a way out. Even when we choose a wrong path, his grace works independent of our choices. In Isaiah the Lord was prophesying about the exile to Babylon because of their rebellion. Yet despite their rejection of the Lord he is going before them to prepare their salvation.

Our hope today is independent of our choices and behaviour. It is not based on our goodness it is based on his goodness. When we are unfaithful the Lord will remain faithful and will continue to work behind the scenes of your life to bring about favour and blessing and lead you into green pastures.

Look at these promises in Isaiah and think about the fullness of grace that has been poured out on us through Jesus. Now we are redeemed through his blood and made righteous. We have had the debt of sin cancelled. How much more can we fully trust and rely on his grace and saving power in our lives?

What a hope we have today! The Lord is moving in your life. He is at work behind the scenes. This is why you can have confidence because he is with you always and he will never leave you.

28

Hope and Joy

Always be prepared to give an answer to everyone who asks you to give the
reason for the hope that you have.

1 Peter 3:15

D o you feel like you are travelling through life at 100 miles per hour? I know personally I like to get things done and I like to see things moving forward but I am learning slowly that it is so important to take time to catch my breath. To stop and reflect about where I am, where I am going and what the Lord is showing me along the way. I think I am realising that life is all about balance. There are some people who are so laid back they are almost horizontal and there are others who are flying through life so fast they are never stopping to enjoy the view!

Have you ever slowed down enough to think about the things that were troubling you last year? The situations or circumstances that you were bringing to the Lord. The niggling doubts that crept into your mind and at times stole your peace. For some of us we can't even remember them which shows us that they were not as troublesome as we had anticipated and we had no need to be concerned about them. For others we can look back with thanks and see how the Lord intervened on our behalf. How he healed us, restored us, delivered us and brought us through. We might not have known all the answers but the Lord was faithful. We overcame and we have come out the other side stronger and wiser.

As believers we have this living hope on the inside of us that causes us to hold on and not give up. The life of Jesus lives within us and He is always calling us to lift up our heads and trust in Him. Now many people in the world cannot understand our response to circumstances and they approach the same things that we are faced with crippled by fear and anxiety. Fear of the unknown, fear of failure, fear of rejection, fear of being abandoned, fear of being truly known, fear of not having enough. .... the list goes on.

Many people will not be able to understand the hope that you have... so tell them who it is based on. Jesus came to set the captives free and now His spirit lives within us and He is calling us to share this hope of freedom and life with the people in our worlds.

As I have looked back over the time in lockdown I can see so many of the positives that have been a blessing on our family. Our lives had been strippped back but it had forced us to look at our priorities. The Lord has shown me how much of my time was spent on things that didn't actually bring me life. Even with our kids we re- evaluated the things they spent their time doing and looked at what was really important. Was being part of lots of clubs more important than spending time together as a family.

The Lord showed us new ways to work, new opportunities for our business, new schedules for our weeks and the importance of taking time out to be refreshed and renewed. In all the uncertainty and disruption our hope was in the Lord's ability to lead and guide us. We didn't fear because we knew he would protect us and provide a way through even when we didn't know what that would look like.

I love the fact that the Lord is no respecter of persons. What He will do for me He will do for all His people. What an incredible difference we could have in this world if we as believers could share this confidence and faith with those around us.

These verses in Genesis bring me such an assurance when I am faced with a challenging situation.

You intended to harm me, but God intended it for good to accomplish what is now being done, the saving of many lives (Genesis 50:20).

This is why we can have hope to share with those around us. The Lord wants to bring people out of fear to a life of confidence and peace for the future. Every trial and difficult situation he will turn around and what the enemy meant for evil, He will turn to blessing and joy!

29

We will Flourish!

The righteous flourish like the palm tree and grow like a cedar in Lebanon.
They are planted in the house of the Lord; they flourish in the courts of our
God.

Psalm 92:12-13

Psalm 92 is one of my favourite psalms and I love all the imagery in it. Not that I am a great gardener but I love the pictures it gives of the trees and what it means to be planted in God's house.

I have learnt that nothing is in the Bible by chance so when I read today's verse I asked myself why is the psalmist talking about these particular varieties of trees and what is he teaching us? Why does the Lord choose the palm tree? What is it that we can learn when we think of this picture the Lord is painting for us?

The palm tree can grow in a dry, desert place. In fact it can thrive in a climate where other plants would perish. It stands upright among all the trees and it rises tall straight towards heaven. Not only that but it is a fruit bearing tree that provides dates, which are very nutritious. In fact man can survive on dates for a considerable amount of time without any other kind of food. Finally a palm tree is known for its beautiful evergreen foliage.

This is how the Lord wants you to imagine yourself. Whatever circumstance or situation you are in you will thrive. Despite the conditions and how others fare you will be able to flourish. You are fed from a heavenly source that will sustain you and you will be a noticed for your beauty which will point others to their saviour and bring glory to the Lord.

How rich is the word of God. How significant is each detail. The Lord longs for us to delve into the depths of his word and to seek out the treasures he has buried within.

Psalm 92 also talks about the cedar in Lebanon. These particular trees are mentioned a number of times in the Bible. David used them for building his palace and Solomon used them for building the temple. They were regarded as an item of luxury and wealth, an abundance of Cedar was a sign of prosperity. The Cedar tree was considered to be the strongest and they were chosen for their size, durability and beauty. They also had a pleasant fragrance. Another detail that I found particularly interesting is that they are resistant to decay and bugs.

So this is how the Lord says we will grow- like the Cedar of Lebanon. We will be strong, durable, an object of beauty. We will not be subject to decay instead we will be a picture of stability and will emit the fragrance of the Lord.

How many of us are allowing the word to transform our thinking so that instead of feeling weak and defeated we can see ourselves as the Lord has made us to be - strong, secure, prosperous and beautiful. This is not wishful thinking. This is truth.

And a final word of encouragement from this psalm is in verse 14 - *They still bear fruit in old age; they are ever full of sap and green.*

This is the Lord's promise over our lives. We go from glory to glory. We don't have to fear old age but instead we can belief for the Lord's supernatural strength within us. What incredible hope for today and our tomorrow.

30

Your greatest treasure

I consider your Word to be my greatest treasure, and I treasure it in my heart

Psalm 119:11

When we embark on this journey of saturating our minds with the truth of who God is and what he has done for us we will find that we are anchoring ourselves to the eternal hope for our lives.

This is the Lord's desire for us. That His word is a life giving source that has such an impact on our lives that we treasure it - *The words you speak to me are worth more than all the riches and wealth in the whole world!* (Psalm 119:72).

It would be easy to dismiss the psalms and think the writers didn't know what real life was like. To suppose that they didn't face the kind of challenges that we have to struggle with everyday. However, nothing could be further from the truth. In the psalms we find the writers encountering moments of grief, turmoil and despair, when they cry out to God as if all hope is lost but then they bring themselves back to the word of the Lord and fix their eyes on what it says - *Lord, I'm fading away. I'm discouraged and lying in the dust revive me by your word, just like you promised you would.* (Psalm 119:25).

The reality that we face everyday is that we are living in a broken world. The effects of the fall are all around us. There is evil and death and the consequences of sin, yet the Lord wants to show us that we will not be overcome. As new covenant believers we stand in the finished work of Jesus.

The psalmist knew this battle of being surrounded by problems and feeling the overwhelming emotions that come with all of that and yet he had an unshakable hope knowing that the answer would be found in the word - "*My life's strength melts away with grief and sadness; come strengthen me and encourage me with your words.*"(Psalm 119:28).

The word strengthens us, the word encourages us, the word will show us a way forward. Although there are going to be trials and hard times, we will get through them because we have one who is faithful and trustworthy.

The Lord wants us to be fully persuaded about where our hope comes from and he wants to ensure that we are firmly established in the truth that we need to help us not only endure but to come out from tribulations declaring that we are more than conquerors.

So many people today are chasing after all the wrong things believing that they will find the keys to happiness. For some it is about position. Being significant through their accomplishments, promotion or reputation. For others it is all about attaining wealth and believing material things will fill the void inside. And finally there are those that look to their popularity and social circle. Whatever it maybe these things will appear to be the answer to our deepest desires but they will never truly satisfy. We will be left feeling short changed because they fail to deliver what we expected.

This is what David discovered and what he shares with us. David had known what it was like to be poor and destitute and rejected. He had also experienced all the riches of life as a king and yet look at what he esteems most- his greatest treasure in life was having God's word - *O how I love and treasure your law; throughout the day I fill my heart with its light!* (Psalm 119:97).

If we want to live a life filled with hope then we will find it through a relationship with Jesus and a life that fixes our thoughts on the promises of His word.

About the Author

Penny has been involved in ministry for over 25 years. She currently lives in Belfast where she is married with 3 great kids. With her husband she founded Exchange Church Belfast, a church family that is committed to seeing the world transformed by the grace of God. She is a certified Executive Coach and facilitator working with some of the world's biggest brands providing leadership and management development programmes. A gifted speaker and leader, Penny uses her experience as a pastor, wife & mother to connect people to the truth of God's love and grace.

You can connect with me on:

🌐 https://www.exchangechurchbelfast.com

Subscribe to my newsletter:

✉ https://www.exchangechurchbelfast.com/devotional